AS ANGELS WATCH

AS ANGELS WATCH

Hazel S. Milnor

Aloha —

Hazel S. Milnor

VANTAGE PRESS
New York

FIRST EDITION

Published by Vantage Press, Inc.
516 West 34th Street, New York, New York 10001

Manufactured in the United States of America
ISBN: 0-533-12159-0

Library of Congress Catalog Card No.: 96-90749

0 9 8 7 6 5 4 3 2 1

For Mary and Jean Ann

"For they shall all know me, from the least of them to the greatest of them, saith the Lord."
—Jeremiah 31:34

All funds to author, from the sale of this book, are for nondenominational religious education for persons with mental retardation.

As angels watch
    the life flow
Of earth's revolving sphere
    from birth of earth
To human growth
    and all life dwelling here,
Of life's rotating seasons
    changes all soon know
As future merges with the past
    in one continuous flow
Of challenges, changes, renewal,
    with discards left behind
As angels watch . . . forever near,
    their seasons . . . infinite time.

Contents

PART III
IN PRAISE OF EARTH

PART IV
HEAVENLY MUSING

AS ANGELS WATCH

Poetic
Writing and Sayings
In Praise of
God . . . Angels . . . Earth

PART I

IN PRAISE OF GOD

MYSTERY

We stretch our mind
    to comprehend
The mystery of God
    and angels
As life's journey astounds,
    confounds and abounds
With wonders unfolding
    around us.
Each molecule, each space,
    galaxy, woman or man,
Reflects a supreme creative
    force . . . a universal plan.

CREATION

Out of the universe
    a vast space devoid of light
Came the Words of creation
    Words of love, power, and might.
In the six days of creation
    God made heaven and earth
The seas, land, and light,
    The sun, moon, and stars were created
And—all forms of life.

THE HOLY LAND

A rugged land
    of contrasts and depths,
From arid sand
    and the Dead Sea
To fertile lands,
    mountains, trees.
From this small land
    came a special relation
With God and angels,
    prophets . . . and salvation.
Three paths to God
    were left in this land
Sacred to Judaism,
    Christianity, and Islam.

THE WALL

A towering limestone wall,
    symbol of religion, power, and pillage,
With crevices between the stones
    serving as repositories of notes,
Messages of praise, thanksgiving, and petition
    for the eyes of "the one God."
The "Temple Wall," the "Western Wall,"
    the "Wailing Wall" becoming the "Happy Wall"
As tears for sorrows past are followed
    by tears for joys present,
By processions, celebrations, religious
    ritual dancing and bar mitzvahs,
In one shining moment at this wall—all
    honor God and a religion rooted in antiquity,
While sending out tendrils for future blossoms,
    as through the centuries . . . the angels watch.

SUPREME REALITY

In love, praise, petition, fear
    we are bold to say
The word "God"
    the supreme reality, creator
Of all that is visible, invisible.
    We read in sacred texts
Of one of unlimited authority,
    always in all places
With understanding of all things,
    omnipotent, omnipresent, omniscient,
The totality of the being
    we worship, may elude us,
But with faith we are one
    in the mystery . . . in the glory of God.

CHOICE

War in heaven ended in a rout
    with Satan the devil and
His angels cast out,
    a very wrong choice by Adam & Eve
Found them hiding behind
    a cluster of leaves,
Cast out of Eden
    and onto the earth,
To toil and suffer pain in childbirth.
    As in heaven and Eden
Choices determine our way
    the wisdom of sacred texts
May guide our earth stay.
    Moses' "Laws," "Ten Commandments,"
Jesus' "Sacrifice," Commandments Two.
    Muhammad changed a nation
With the Koran and example, too.
    Jews, Christians, and Islam
Worship "One God" . . . Monotheism.
    Believe in angels, right decisions
To attain paradise, heaven.

LOVE

Experiencing a detachment,
    lost in our own time zone,
Realizing a deepening feeling
    for a special one we know,
And an illusion, tranquil fantasy,
    paints our world a rosy glow
With exquisite kaleidoscopic weather,
    and a stunning rainbow
While a mosiac of emotions,
    passes the screen of our mind
With a mix of hope and dreams,
    and an invisible tie that binds.
This supreme blessing of God,
    This divinc gift from above
Fuels the continuity of life
    as unconditional love.

BEAUTY

Refreshing as dew
    on a flower
Is love to the spirit
    of man,
Nurturing essential
    for the flower
Also essential for
    woman and man.
God's love for His
    earth creations
Received as spirit
    or dew . . .
Gives us the beauty of nature,
    and spiritual beauty, too.

PERSPECTIVE

The excitement of a moonwalk
    a view of earth from space,
The miracles of medicine,
    a computer-generated pace,
There are the "black holes" of astronomy
    and for space and global sounds
There's communication . . . and TV
    with such wonders earth abounds,
But to create an earth or heaven,
    or a human from rib or dust
Returns us to sacred texts,
    for such creations, God is a must.

STORM CLOUDS

When ominous clouds
  are hovering near
When adversity and disasters
  are what we most hear
When wars and mistakes
  bring numbing fear
We may cry,
  "God, spare me."
Whether we curse
  and then start to flee
Whether we stand
  tall as a tree,
Whether we pause,
  on bended knee,
We may cry,
  "God, help me . . . please,"
With humility, faith
  and prayers rife
With joining the spiritual
  flow of all life, then
with newfound grace,
  for meeting life's strife,
We may cry,
  "God, we thank thee."

REASSURANCE

The questions of life,
 the reason for being,
Of angels, the universe, man
 sought in sacred texts
And historical drama seeking
 God's overall plan.
With earth's grandeur . . .
 and universality
Mixed with the whirl
 of land and sea
And the actions of
 individual elements
What a plan this has to be.
 Pausing, gazing, at the night sky
Our thoughts . . . roam free
 through the incredible universe
And timeless eternity.
 Becoming still . . . we wonder
How does this relate to me?
 Then remembering creation's history
And God's love calms fear
 of the questions and the mystery
Of this life . . . and why we're here.

THE KINGDOMS

History is recorded
    in the endless flow of time,
Knowledge is imprinted
    in the corridors of the mind
From the kingdom of God within
    comes love—of God and humankind
From the kingdom of God above
    comes love—and everlasting life.

HEAVENLY HEALING

The desolation of your separation
    and the blackness of your loss
Are brightened with the knowledge
    of God, angels, and the cross.
Soothing, gentle healing,
    the heavenly help given all
Brings renewal and peace of spirit,
    blessed strength and the wherewithal
To endure . . . and triumph.

TAKE A LOOK

Take a look around you
    and you will see
How God has provided
    for such as we
A planet, with the potential
    for all we would be
And a Book for guidelines
    with our choices—free.
Take a look around you
    and pause—thought free
For a "thank you" for just being,
    and for all you see.

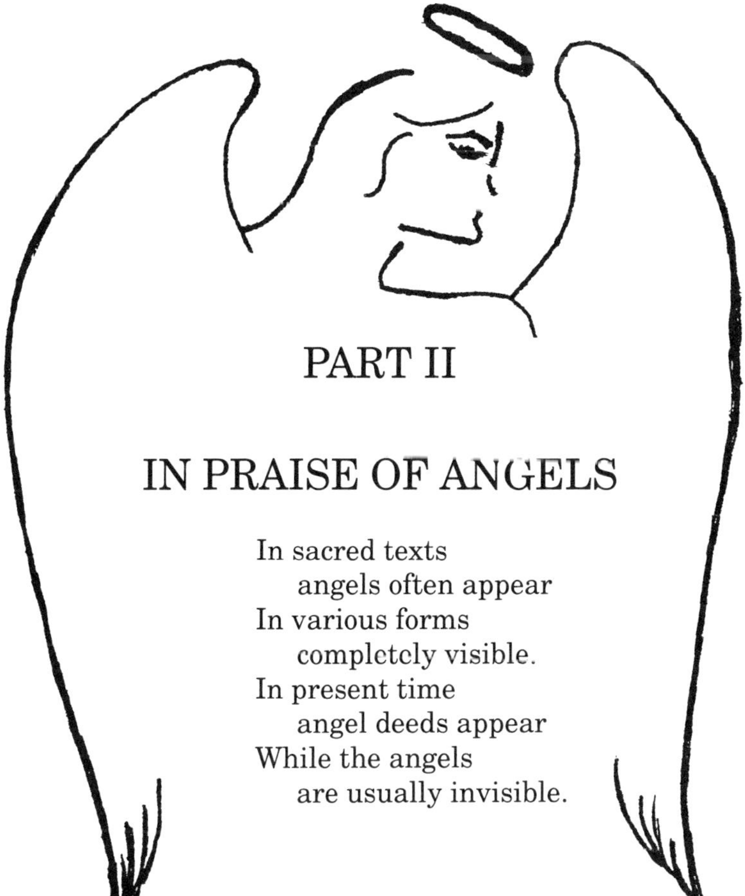

PART II

IN PRAISE OF ANGELS

In sacred texts
    angels often appear
In various forms
    completely visible.
In present time
    angel deeds appear
While the angels
    are usually invisible.

ANGELS

Young . . . as the believer,
    older than time
Celestial angels . . .
    terrestrial, divine
With messages and deeds
    imprinting history
While traversing the universe
    in an aura of mystery
As spiritual beings
    of another time and sphere,
Even as the Creator they serve,
    so removed . . . yet . . . so near.

ANGEL JOURNEY

Angels, spirits catapulted
    through time and space
Riding the point of an
    arrow of thought.
No vapor trail, no twinkling
    blink of light
Trailing through the universe,
    as angels move
Silently and swiftly
    out of heaven to earth.
Then mission accomplished
    a return to heaven
Leaving earth to ponder
    the mystery of angels.

ANGEL—TIME

Some moments, intervals
    of present time,
Seem an eternity
    sometimes,
But time may seem
    a blink of the eye
While glancing back
    at years gone by . . .
At history of man and nations
    blossoming before decline,
But "God's Word" and angels
    transcend space and time.

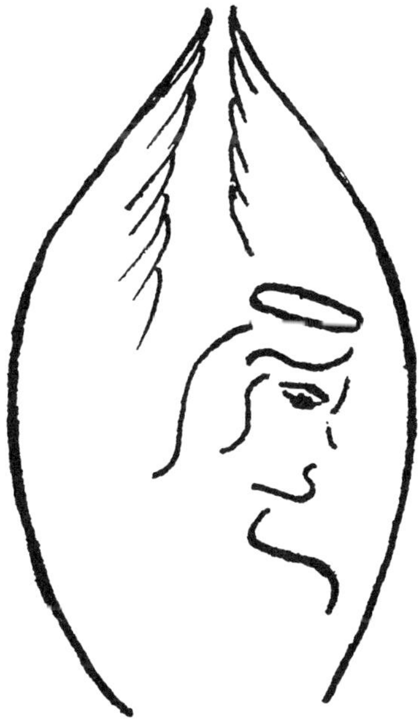

GUARDIAN ANGEL

A caressingly soft breeze,
    a glitter of light
Reminds me my angel is
    just out of sight,
Moving silent as a shadow
    and swifter than light
My celestial connection
    and sentinel divine . . .
Loving thanks, guardian angel
    for "special care" through time.

ARCHANGELS

Impressive deeds portrayed
    and faultlessly acted roles,
Starring archangels accorded
    most awesome goals.
Diplomatic communicators,
    in heaven and earth
Warriors, teachers, healers,
    messengers of birth.
And for Him, from whose Word
    they were initially cast,
Is given unconditional love
    and loyalty unsurpassed
By the archangels, chief angels,
    heavenly help . . . future and past.

GABRIEL

(I)

With dazzling glitter,
    and Christmas tree lights,
With feasting and gifts
    there's joy . . . and delight.
But, a decorative angel
    causes pause for thought
Of the special message
    that Gabriel brought
Foretelling to Mary
    The Holy Birth,
Celebrated at Christmas
    around planet Earth.

GABRIEL

(II)

Winds of change
    renew the earth
Through ages and cycles
    of time and birth,
To Muhammad in Saudi Arabia
    Gabriel brought a command
Changing religion and culture
    through Allah and Islam.

MICHAEL

Fabled lands of deserts,
    camels and sheep
Of princes and swift horses
    passing beggars at city gates.
And in troubled times,
    the heavenly help of Michael
And his angels,
    their heroic deeds prevailing
In heaven and on Earth, sacred
    texts tell us.

RAPHAEL—TOBIT, SARAH

From two in exile
    fervent prayers arose,
And an angel received a commission,
    compassionate healing
A wedding and feasting ensued
    following Raphael's mission.

ANGEL MORONI

Out of radiant light
    heavenly help intercedes,
Bringing man truth
    and religious seed,
With divine guidance
    and man's deeds
A church emerged
    fulfilling a need.

FAITH

Shadrach, Meshach, and Abednego,
    devout in Babylon of old,
Refused when King Nebuchadnezzar
    demanded worship of an idol of gold.
Faith in their own God was earnest
    and an angel, heavenly help from above,
Delivered them from the furnace,
    to worship the God
Shadrach, Meshach, and Abednego loved.

WHEEL OF TIME

Angels move through the universe,
    past galaxies, through heavens divine,
Through millennia and earth cycles,
    with dignity and might sublime,
And with such ease as though turning a
    dial on a mystical "wheel of time"
To place them in the cycle and flow
    as they continue through time.

AN ANGEL'S DAY

Angels pass through the
    invisible mirror, of another
Age, another world
    without dimensional challenges,
From heaven to earth
    and return, leaving
An earth day filled
    with amazement, wonder,
Unbelief, until the reality
    of an event, an unexpected
Happening, transfixes thinking
    and changes a life.

SATAN

The angel by whatever name called
    Abaddon, Apollyn, Izrail, or
Satan, presides over a place
    at the opposite end
Of the spiritual spectrum.
    With a musical symphony
Of shrieks, moans, and groans
    fragrance of the dying
Wafting through the gloom
    of darkness, heat, pain
Famine . . . and more.
    Ghastly hellish hell
A cesspool of abomination
    a place "we abhor."

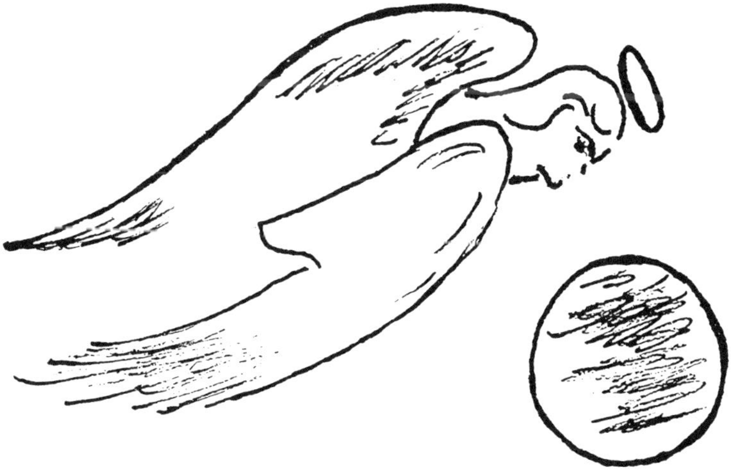

PART III

IN PRAISE OF EARTH

PLANET EARTH

What a celestial celebration,
 such ethereal praise,
As "all the sons of God
 shouted for joy,"
"And the morning stars
 together sang," as the
Foundations of earth were laid.*

 The glory, the magnitude,
The birth of all visible,
 and invisible in this
New revolving sphere,
 filled with choices,
Challenges, discoveries,
 sufficient for the days
Of planet Earth and
 all life here.

*KJV, Job 38:7

BEGINNING OF FOREVER

Earth, an island a microcosm
    in our wondrous universe,
We rejoice and praise
    our time, our space,
Even as the "sons of God,"
    shouted for joy as
The "foundations were laid"
    for the birth of Earth,
Our planet . . . where
    our beginning of forever
Is spent, the result of God,
    Adam and Eve.

MAN AND WOMAN

PROLOGUE

And the Lord God formed man of dust of the ground, and breathed into his nostrils the breath of life; and man became a living soul.

And the Lord God planted a garden eastward in Eden; and there he put the man whom he had formed.

And the rib, which the Lord God had taken from the man, made he a woman, and brought her unto the man.*

And Adam called his wife's name Eve, because she was the mother of all living.**

For gaining knowledge of good and evil, through disobedience and the serpent's temptation, a punishment of pain and toil was placed on humankind. The Lord God cast Adam and Eve out of the garden of Eden. Cherubims, and a turning flaming sword, were placed to keep the way of the tree of life.

*Genesis 2:7, 8, 22, KJV
**Genesis 3:20

A LIFE CYCLE

Male, and female, arrive on planet Earth red of face, fists clenched, and echoing cries of protest for being cast out of the warmth and security of the mother's womb.

With time . . . with growth . . . with knowledge he or she pursues the path of choice . . . a path heavy with temptation.

With time . . . with growth . . . with ability they plant seeds and ascend to the peak of choice.

With time . . . and with diminishing ability he or she descends the peak and rests.

With time . . . and with the body weary the spirit transcends leaving a hollow shell behind . . . with a heritage shadowed by decisions of good deeds . . . or evil.

And ever so the full life cycle of man and woman has been . . . from the creation of Adam and Eve unto the present time.

EPILOGUE

And man and woman return to earth . . . "for out of it wast thou taken: for dust thou art and unto dust shalt thou return."*

And with the winds of time their dust, their seed, their handiwork is scattered upon the face of the universe.

*Genesis 3:19, KJV

THERE IS MORE

Man sought survival and he survived;
    he sought to surpass and he surpassed
And found travel and material possessions,
    but not satisfied he said, "There must
Be more."
    He looked in the mirror and found a
Stranger. He studied the stranger and
    found within
God, heavenly help and the promise of
    life eternal
And man said, "There is more."

SANDPRINTS

The sapphire blue of deep water
    turns to emerald green near land
And white-crested rolling waves
    wash footprints from the sand,
As man relentlessly pursues his journey
    on land, in space, and through the sea
Rarely leaving more to mark his passage
    than footprints we no longer see.
Wherever man roams or wanders
    his destiny a mystery,
What a blessing and comfort to know
    God and angels are with thee.

BROTHERS AND SISTERS?

From whatever continent or island
    whatever color, creed, or race,
Whether Buddhist, Hindu, Muslim,
    Jew, Christian, or other faith,
But with something special in common,
    as belief in a Power unseen,
A Power with unique helpers
    in physical or spiritual mien.
Does that make us brothers and
    sisters, revering the same Power
Supreme, sharing seed of the Adam
    and Eve tree while continuing the
Life-flowing stream?

PAINTED MOUNTAINS

From silence to roaring
    atop barren peaks
As winds paint with snowflakes
    the mountains become streaked,
Gentle winds become gales
    of great turbulent might
Dropping snowflakes in mounds
    from each swirling flight.
The raging storm blows over,
    blustery winds, such magnitude,
Leave white majestic mountains
    to the quiet of solitude . . .
Watched by angels.

OCEAN FASCINATION

The fascination of the ocean
    the charm of a calm sea
Rolling waves liquid beauty
    lulling, calling one to see
Their world below the surface,
    giant fish flashing bright
Myriad treasures under water
    in a world of soft twilight.
While sunlight fades on the surface
    as a raging typhoon descends
With a howl, the clap of thunder,
    mountainous water pours in
As giant waves splinter timber
    sending objects galore
From the churning, heaving surface
    to the ocean's rocky floor
Littering shipwrecks, broken pieces,
    dishes, stacks, an unhinged door
Create adventure for the fish
    and future people to explore,
The fascination of the ocean
    enjoyed, transversed . . . utilized
Probing watery space around us
    each new aspect scrutinized.
Yet some secrets of the oceans
    When created? Why sublime?
Leave generations to ponder
    with the answers . . . perhaps in time.

STALWART TREES

The beauty, the splendor
    of mammoth stalwart trees
As faded growth drops
    in heaps of fallen leaves.
Such beauty, such color
    by the creator all were cast
And glorify the pathway
    of those who wander past.
Their comfort, their shelter
    For journeyer or stray
Cause some to pause and wonder
    to linger, to stay.
Their branches sway and bow
    to nature's awesome swaths
Of rain, snow, and winds that blow
    in unrelenting blasts.
The beauty, the splendor
    of mammoth stalwart trees,
Reflecting life in nature
    with God-given ease.

EARTH'S TREASURES

A clear pool of water
 reflecting sunlight
In a kaleidoscope of colors,
 a magical sight!
May this fleeting moment
 be etched in your mind
With life's special memories
 of treasures in time.

BLESSED

A crimson gold sunset
    painting a palm-fringed sea,
The scent of perfume from
    plants and flowering trees,
A chilled drink shared with friends,
    friends—two or three,
A feast—of the senses
    how blessed life can be.

PART IV

HEAVENLY MUSING

HEAVENLY MUSING

On the gently moving water
    shimmering moonlight
Forms golden pathways
    to the heavens
Making a joyful slide
    for angels
And a gilded pathway
    for man's thoughts to climb,
The magnificence of such beauty
    giving pause and reflection . . .
How can anyone doubt
    the creator of it all?

THE DANCER . . . SALOME?

As soft-stringed music echoes
 through the massive hall
The sensuous dancer twirls and drops
 a perfumed veil, quite small—
Amid chatter, laughter, and flirtations
 spirits and wine served to all
As burning torches cast shadows
 that flicker on palace walls.
Why this dazzling assemblage of people
 seeking pleasure in the palace hall?
A king is providing lavish feasting for
 rulers of principalities, powers all.
But heavenly help is much needed
 at this gala hedonistic ball
As diabolically evil ones lurk about
 plotting man's ultimate fall.

ANGEL LIGHT

May angels of heaven weave
    a tapestry of celestial light,
With gold of sun, silver of moon,
    and sparkle of soft starlight,
For a mystical, magical cover
    to envelop the earth at night
In a heavenly glow . . . for a time of peace
    while basking in angel light.

NATURE'S SYMPHONY

The sounds of wind swaying
    the branches of trees,
And the lapping of shore water,
    float on the breeze
For the magic, of nature's symphony,
    to soothe and to please.
And the fluttering of wings
    as angels pass,
Accenting the birds' singing
    for this spiritual repast
Of nature's symphony with guest artists
    for music unsurpassed.

THE SEARCH

From thoughtful depths . . .
    "Why—this journey on planet Earth?"
Echoing through the stillness,
    "For love, for woman, for man . . .
A choice of destiny."
And . . .
    "Why this restless search for peace?"
The words, gentle as a caressing breeze:
    "All one seeks . . .
Is found within."

REJOICING

When lead gray skies bring snow flurries
drifting high in mounds of white
Do angels rejoice in happy frolicking
white-flecked wings a streak of light
Turning, tumbling like windblown snowflakes
cavorting as they race in flight
Joyfully doing His commandments
for heavenly help, miracles of might?

RESPITE

Happiness, an oasis in time
    as thoughts float free
Merging with magical expectations
    of endless peace, joy, love.
Happiness, recognizing nature's gifts
    as a clear-tinkling stream
The aura, the magic
    of the moon's luminescence.
Happiness, an interval oblivious of time,
    while on an irreversible course
To the end . . . of Earth's reality,
    as angels watch.

HEAVENLY HELP

The moon is dark and raindrops splatter
as gusts of wind put leaves in flight,
Our angel friends—work harder
on a windy, starless, rain-soaked night.
But whether your thoughts are bright and
sunny or troubled and dark as a stormy night,
Rest assured . . . heavenly help is always near
as you journey through this life.

STAR WISH

An opulent night sky,
    sparkling with stars
Filling the serene silence
    with harmony and repose.
Then a "star wish,"
    "To pass through
    the cosmic divide
    to a heaven where angels sing.
    A special moment
    in timeless time
    viewing saints, immortals
    and all the divine."
This dream of a wish—
    leaving Earth's reality
In spirit form only
    not physical totality
Just a momentary break
    not infinite finality.

ALWAYS HERE

Illuminated by a canopy
    of full moon and glittering stars
The wretched search through a
    landscape—trashscape of tin
Cans, plastic and litter.
    Amidst urban traffic—carts
Are pushed as others search for
    shelter or a comforting grate.
While in a luxurious dwelling sparkling
    wine accelerates conversation
Among the family viewing TV news . . .
    the latest flashes—disasters,
Violence and skeletal apparitions
    of the starving. Conversation slows,
Stops, appalled one viewer mutters,
    "Why isn't something done for these
People?" "Where is God?" With a
    shake of head, another says, "Human
Compassion is gone . . . not God."
    While another murmurs, "Love thy
Neighbor," "brother's keeper,"
    "And that reminds me, did anyone
Pick up our travel tickets today?"

PARADISE ON EARTH

Lend me eyes to see,
    to see only the beauty of people,
Of nature, and the universe,
    lend me ears to hear
To hear only the music of nature,
    of life, and the earth,
Lend me voice for sound
    for sound only with compassion,
With joy, with mirth,
    lend me the heavenly help of angels
Angels of peace and love,
    for Paradise on Earth!

DANCE OF LIFE

Shadowing the actions of today
    are events of the past,
As spiritual and secular uplink
    forming earth's teeming mass.
While space satellites, space eyes,
    view our revolving sphere,
Our fishbowl in the cosmos,
    as angels watch quite near.
While we drift, turn, frayed
    by purpose, passion, pain
Till the dance of life fades,
    leaving the spirit free
To begin the awesome quest
    of life in eternity.

CHERUBIM, WHEELS, AND SERAPHIM

Challenging our imaging
 of awesome things
The vision of cherubim
 with multiple wings,
And faces like . . .
 cherubs, man, and more
As lion and eagle
 different faces—four.
Also, fearsome wheels
 rising in the air
These wheels alight
 with eyes everywhere.*
And a limitless spectrum
 of heavenly might
Are the six/winged seraphim**
 as lightning in flight,
Their wings folded in reverence
 when standing before
Their creator, the ONE
 they revere and adore.***
These other world beings
 of another time and place
Serve the creator of Earth
 creator of our time and space.

*Ezekial 10:1-20, KJV
**Isaiah 6:2, KJV
***The Zondervan Pictorial Bible Dictionary p.772

WHATEVER HAPPENED TO EDEN?

Whatever happened to Eden,
  known as Paradise to all?
Did it just dematerialize
  following the graceless fall
Of Adam, Eve, and the serpent
  cast outside the wall?
But whatever happened to Eden,
  left remote and unnoted by time,
This garden of idyllic enchantment
  this desire of humankind?
Is it in another dimension
  known on Earth as eternity
Or was it just removed
  with total finality?

THE DOORS

The sun sets
    closing the day
Opening the door
    to night.
Even as death
    closes an Earth journey
Opening the door
    to . . . eternity.

CLAY

Clay touched by God
  became a mortal,
Clay touched by mortal
  returned to dust.
Mortal touched by God
  becomes immortal
With God's touch
  clay transcends dust.

WISDOM

Some call wisdom
    the wife of God.
This requires thought,
    more than a passing nod.
    (metaphorical, allegorical?)
Could wisdom be a wife?
    or an intellectual creation
Endowed in one and all
    for special edification?
    (Solomon?)
As our creator fills the universe
    with power and history
Still so much about God
    is to me a mystery
Including His wisdom.

LEFT BEHIND

I weep for the friend
  no longer with me
Whose challenges in life
  have now been set free.
Memories of your life
  happiness, pain, and tears
Cause my eyes to flow
  remembering the years.
As I weep for my friend
  with tears so free
I know in my heart
  the tears are for me,
For the void in my life
  where you used to be.

At the last
people terrestrial
may become immortal
beings celestial,
and as celestials
they may shine
and along with angels
continue through time.